FAR-OUT and UNUSUAL pets

Hairless Dogs

Cool Pets!

Alvin and Virginia Silverstein
and Laura Silverstein Nunn

Enslow Elementary
an imprint of
E
Enslow Publishers, Inc.
40 Industrial Road
Box 398
Berkeley Heights, NJ 07922
USA
http://www.enslow.com

Enslow Elementary, an imprint of Enslow Publishers, Inc.

Enslow Elementary® is a registered trademark of Enslow Publishers, Inc.

Library of Congress Cataloging-in-Publication Data:

Silverstein, Alvin.
Hairless dogs : cool pets! / Alvin Silverstein, Virginia Silverstein, and Laura Silverstein Nunn.
p. cm. — (Far-out and unusual pets)
Includes index.
Summary: "Provides basic information about hairless dogs and keeping them as pets"—Provided by publisher.
ISBN 978-0-7660-3879-0
1. Hairless dogs—Juvenile literature. I. Silverstein, Virginia B. II. Nunn, Laura Silverstein. III. Title.
SF429.H27S55 2012
636.755—dc22
2011008757

Future editions:
Paperback ISBN 978-1-4644-0124-4
ePUB ISBN 978-1-4645-1031-1
PDF ISBN 978-1-4646-1031-8

Printed in the China

012012 Leo Paper Group, Heshan City, Guangdong, China

10 9 8 7 6 5 4 3 2 1

To Our Readers: We have done our best to make sure all Internet Addresses in this book were active and appropriate when we went to press. However, the author and the publisher have no control over and assume no liability for the material available on those Internet sites or on other Web sites they may link to. Any comments or suggestions can be sent by e-mail to comments@enslow.com or to the address on the back cover.

Photo Credits: © 2011 Photos.com, a division of Getty Images, pp. 8, 23 (bottom); Alamy: © Juniors Bildarchiv, p. 18, © Tierfotoagentur, p. 32; Anton Gvozdikov/Shutterstock.com, p. 11; AP Photo: Karel Navarro, p. 29, Tina Fineberg, p. 36; AP Images/The News Gazette, John Dixon, p. 23 (top); Imagebroker.net/Photolibrary, p. 41; © iStockphoto.com/Paul Gregg, p. 9; Jewel Waldrip, p. 28; © Kolar, Richard/Animals Animals–Earth Scenes, p. 39; MARIANA BAZO/Reuters /Landov, p. 44; ROSIE HALLAM/MCT/Landov, p. 19; Shutterstock.com, pp. 3, 4, 6, 13, 15, 21, 26; © The Trustees of the British Museum/Art Resource, NY, p. 10.

Cover Photo: Shutterstock.com

Contents

Hairless dogs can be really great pets!

1

Hairless Wonders

When you think of a far-out and unusual pet, a dog probably doesn't even enter your mind. After all, dogs are the most popular pets in America! But what about a dog that doesn't have fur? Now *that* would be unusual.

Dogs are known for their fur coats, so one look at a hairless dog can be pretty shocking. It looks like someone has shaved off the fur from its body. But hairless dogs don't get their unusual looks from a fancy haircut. This is just the way they are.

Despite their name, hairless dogs are not completely hairless. There are different kinds

This Chinese Crested dog has fur in a few places, but it is still considered a hairless dog.

(breeds) of hairless dogs. Most of them do have some hair. In fact, one popular hairless breed has thick tufts of fur on the dog's head, ears, tail, and paws. The rest of the body is bare. Some breeds may look hairless, but they actually have tiny hairs covering their body.

Hairless dogs are becoming popular pets. Pet owners say to know them is to love them. Hairless dogs are just as sweet and lovable as any other dog pet. Besides, what could be better than a dog that doesn't shed? No dog hair on clothes, furniture, or the carpet!

Keeping any dog is a big responsibility. But hairless dogs need a little extra special care. Without fur, their body needs to be protected from the hot sun or chilly weather.

Read on to find out what makes hairless dogs such far-out and unusual pets.

When it is cold outside, hairless dogs need help keeping warm.

Got a Dog Allergy?

Achoo! Every time you go near a dog, you start sniffling and sneezing. Your eyes itch and you just feel miserable. You might think that owning a hairless dog would solve that pesky dog allergy problem. Actually, it is not the dog's hair that makes you sneeze or get itchy red eyes. Dog allergies are caused mainly by dander—dead flakes of skin!

Although many hairless dogs do not have any fur, they do have dander. However, hairless dogs tend to shed less dander than furry dogs. But still, even a hairless dog is not allergy-proof. To be sure, spend time with the dog before you adopt it.

2

Ready for a Hairless Dog?

"What happened to its coat?" That's usually people's first reaction when they see a hairless dog. Many people don't know that hairless dogs even exist. But this is not some new breed of dog. Hairless dogs have been around for over 3,000 years! Statues and paintings of them were found in the tombs of ancient Egyptians. The Egyptians thought hairless dogs had healing powers.

This pottery figure of a hairless dog was made in Colima, Mexico, about 2,000 years ago. According to ancient myths, such dogs helped the dead travel to the underworld.

These hairless dogs are competing in a dog show.

These dogs were worshipped by everyone, but only royalty and the rich owned them.

Throughout history, hairless dogs appeared in paintings and other works of art. They were also described in many books. By the late 1800s, these hairless wonders competed in dog shows. They made quite a stir with their unusual looks. Soon many people took these fascinating dogs into their households and made them a part of their family. Over the years, hairless dogs have become increasingly popular pets.

Far Out!

The Healing Touch

People once believed that hairless dogs were a cure for aches and pains. A dog's normal body temperature is about 102 F (39 C). That's higher than the normal temperature for people (98.6 F or 37 C). Without fur, a hairless dog's body feels really warm to the touch. The warmth of the dog's body feels good on a person's aching body part. The dog's body acts like a heating pad. Hairless dogs slept in their owners' beds. Besides helping to relieve aches and pains, the hairless dogs were great bed-warmers on cold nights.

This hairless dog has colored patterns on its skin, like the markings on a furry dog's hair.

Hairless Dogs Up Close

Hairless dogs come in a variety of colors and patterns. But because they don't have a furry coat, the colors show up on their skin, like a tattoo. The skin can be a solid color, pink with "freckles," patches of color, striped, or spotted in any color combination.

In some hairless breeds, the skin on the dog's head looks very wrinkled. Many furry dogs have wrinkled heads, too. You don't notice the wrinkles on those dogs because they are covered by fur.

Types of Hairless Dogs

There is more than one type of hairless dog breed. In fact, there are over twenty-five of them! Here are some of the most popular breeds people keep as pets:

The *Chinese Crested* is the most well-known type. These are small dogs, weighing 7 to 12 pounds (3.2 to 5.4 kg). This dog looks like a punk rocker. Long, silky hair covers the head (known as

Chinese Cresteds

a crest), tail (plume), and feet (socks). Only the body is free of hair. A Chinese Crested dog has a spunky personality. It is playful, loving, and carefree.

Some Chinese Crested dogs have a full coat of hair. These furry dogs are called Powderpuffs. They can be born in the same litter as hairless

Far Out!

Why Don't Hairless Dogs Have Hair?

It all comes down to genes. Genes are chemicals found in each body cell. They are passed down from parents to their babies. In all living things, these chemicals control what features they will have, such as eye or hair color. Most dogs have genes for short or long hair. Hairless dogs came about because long ago these genes changed somehow. The changed genes created a new kind of dog, one that was missing most or all of its hair. Eventually, different kinds of hairless dogs developed.

In most cases, only one parent must have a gene for hairlessness to have a litter of hairless puppies. However, it is common to have both coated and hairless puppies in the same litter.

Cresteds. Coated or not, these dogs are still the same breed.

The *Mexican Hairless* is another popular breed. It is also known as Xoloitzcuintli (or Xolo for short). You pronounce it "show-low-eats-queen-tlee." This is a very sturdy dog. It has a sleek body, a long neck, almond-shaped eyes, and large bat ears.

There are two varieties of this breed, coated and hairless. The hairless type has a tuft of short, thin hair on the head and neck, feet, and tail tip. There are also three sizes, toy, miniature (mid-size), and standard. The toy size weighs 5 to 13 pounds (2.3 to 5.9 kg), the miniature weighs 13 to 30 pounds (5.9 to 13.6 kg), and the standard weighs 20 to 40 pounds (9 to 18 kg).

The *American Hairless Terrier* is a hairless version of the Rat Terrier. This is a rather recent breed. The first American Hairless Terrier was born in 1972. Unlike other hairless breeds, *both* parents must have a hairless gene to have hairless puppies. These dogs are totally hairless except for

This Mexican Hairless dog has very little fur.

These Hairless Terriers look like they have no fur at all!

their whiskers and eyebrows. There is no hair on their feet, head, or tail. The American Hairless Terrier may weigh between 9 and 20 pounds (4 and 9 kg).

The *Hairless Khala* is another type. *Khala* is an Indian word meaning "without clothing." The dog has a tuft of hair on its head and some hairs on the face. This breed has two interesting varieties: short-legged and long-legged. The Hairless Khala is usually loving and caring toward its owners. But it is known to be unfriendly to strangers. The dog also has an interesting habit. When it gets startled, it freezes (stays very still). The Hairless Khala weighs 15 to 30 pounds (6.8 to 13.6 kg).

The *Peruvian Inca Orchid* is the largest of the hairless breeds. These dogs weigh anywhere from 26 to 50 pounds (11.8 to 22.7 kg). They have thin hair on top of their head, and sometimes on the ears. But the rest of the body is bare.

Far Out!

Flea-Free!

Hairless dogs generally do not get fleas. Fleas like to cling to the dog's furry coat. But most hairless dogs don't have enough hair for them to grab.

Peruvian Inca Orchid

Where Do You Buy a Hairless Dog?

Can you get a hairless dog from a pet store? Probably not. Hairless dogs are usually sold by breeders. Breeders are people who raise animals. You can find many breeders by searching on the Internet with a parent. It is important to make sure you choose a responsible breeder. Otherwise, you may end up with an unfriendly dog. Even worse, the dog may have health problems.

How do you know if a breeder is good? Responsible breeders take special care of their animals. They keep an eye on them and make sure they stay healthy. They also spend time with them to make sure they are friendly. Breeders can also give you information on the puppy's background. In fact, you might even be able to meet the parents. Breeders can also answer any questions you might have.

Here's a helpful tip: If a breeder seems to want a quick sale with no questions asked, stay away! A responsible breeder will ask questions about your

Breeders want to be sure that their dogs will be well taken care of and loved.

family's ideas of raising dogs. Where will the dog sleep? Will it be tied up outside or will it be an indoor dog? How much time will you be able to spend with the dog? All this information will help the breeder decide if you and your family will be responsible pet owners. Generally, good breeders want to place their dogs in homes where the animals will be safe, healthy, and happy.

3

Caring for a Hairless Dog

Have you ever seen dogs dressed in little outfits? The owners are not trying to play dress-up with their pets. (At least, not usually!) They are trying to protect their dogs from the cold weather outside.

Dogs with furry coats can usually handle chilly temperatures. Their thick coat acts like a warm blanket. But some short-haired dogs cannot handle the cold very well. Their coats are not thick enough to hold in heat. So can you imagine what it must be like for a hairless dog? Without a warm blanket of fur, a hairless dog can get really chilled in cool weather. You will have to get your dog some dog sweaters for chilly days and nights.

Dog clothes are important for hairless dogs, especially in cold weather!

All the Comforts of Home

Hairless dogs are *not* outside dogs. They should not be kept in a dog house or tied to a tree outside. It is true that they do like the sun's warmth. But they should not spend long periods of time outside.

Far Out!

A Healthy Tan for Dogs?

Hairless dogs often like to sit out in the sun. The warmth of the sun feels really good on their bare skin. By the end of the summer, many hairless dogs have a suntan. Owners say that a nice suntan makes their pets look healthier and more attractive. However, if a hairless dog stays out in the sun too long, it can get a painful sunburn. Hairless dogs should always wear sunscreen—just as people do—to protect themselves from the sun's burning rays. It is a good idea if they spend small amounts of time out in the sun. That way they can develop a suntan gradually.

During the winter, hairless dogs spend most of the time indoors. So their suntan gradually fades away. Their skin may look pale and washed out. Some people use sun lamps in the winter to help their dogs keep their summer glow.

While your hairless dog may sleep in a regular dog bed, it will also enjoy sleeping next to you.

Do hairless dogs need a special place to sleep? A nice soft dog bed would do just fine. But don't be surprised if your hairless dog prefers to sleep where you are. It will probably snuggle underneath the covers where it is nice and warm.

During the day, your dog needs exercise. Exercise is very important. It helps keep your pet healthy. Dogs that exercise are less likely to become overweight. They also are less likely to become lazy. A fenced-in backyard can give your dog enough room to run around and explore. It is also a good idea to take your dog on walks regularly. Not only is it great exercise, but it is also a way to spend some time with your dog.

Home Alone

Hairless dogs don't like to be left alone for long periods of time. They will get bored and lonely. "My dog ate my homework" is not a joke. If you leave your homework out with a new puppy around, don't be surprised to find it in pieces when you get home.

Why do dogs chew on everything? Dogs are naturally curious animals. They want to check things out. Dogs are like young children. They learn about something by putting it in their mouth.

Then they chew it up. They can feel the texture and the taste when they are chewing. It's their way of exploring.

Dogs—especially puppies—will chew on whatever is around. Your dog doesn't know it has chosen your favorite shoes to chew on. It just knows they're there and are fun to chew. If you aren't going to be home, you should put anything at risk out of the dog's reach. It may help to close the door to your bedroom. Just like a little child, puppies don't always have the self-control to stay away from things that they should not touch.

You can help keep your dog from getting bored by giving it dog toys to play with. They can be squeaky toys, dog ropes, chew toys, and stuffed animals. Show them that it is good to chew on these things. Play with the toys and let the dog bite on them. Leave these toys out when you won't be home. You can keep the dog toys in a special "toy box." Your dog will learn where to go to get some fun toys to play with. Make sure you get a variety,

Hairless dogs love playing with their toys—especially if you are playing, too.

Far Out!

Missing Teeth

Hairless dogs often have problems with their teeth. They may have missing teeth and short teeth roots. (Roots help to anchor teeth deep into the gums.) As the dog gets older, its teeth are likely to fall out. In fact, it is actually rare for hairless dogs to keep all their teeth in old age. However, American Hairless Terriers don't usually have tooth problems. These dogs have a full set of teeth. They keep them all their lives—as long as the teeth are cared for.

so the dog won't get tired of playing with the same thing all the time. (Never give your dog old shoes to chew on. You're saying it's all right to eat shoes. Your dog won't know the difference between a pair of old tennis shoes and your brand new ones.)

It's Chow Time!

Hairless dogs do not need a special diet. They eat the same kind of dog food as other dogs. Dog food you buy in the store is fine. However, make sure it is healthy. Many people think dogs should have a

While hairless dogs can eat any type of dog food, talk to a veterinarian to find out how much food to feed your dog.

meat-only diet. Actually, they should eat a variety of foods. That includes fruits and vegetables. Some favorite fruits may be apple slices, pears, or oranges. Vegetables may include carrots, broccoli, and celery. Eggs are also a healthy food choice for dogs. Many dog foods now add some of these items for a more balanced meal. Don't overfeed your dog, however. Even a healthy diet can make a dog overweight if it eats too much. You should be able to see your dog's waist. Also make sure your pet has fresh water at all times.

Do Hairless Dogs Need Grooming?

A hairless dog means no grooming, right? Actually, no. Even though hairless dogs don't have much hair, they still need to be cleaned and cared for.

A dog's skin produces oils, which normally soak into its fur. These oils help keep the skin soft and prevent it from drying out. But a hairless dog doesn't have fur. So these oils may build up on its skin. The skin may feel sticky. House dirt will start

It is important to keep your hairless dog clean and to keep its skin free of dirt.

Far Out!

My Dog Has Pimples!

A common problem for hairless dogs is acne. That's just a fancy word for pimples! Dogs have pores (openings) in their skin just like people do. Oils pour out of the pores in the skin. But when they build up, the pores can get clogged. Bacteria (germs) can grow and multiply in clogged pores. Then the dogs' skin starts to break out in little pimples. Often skin problems get worse when dogs wear sweaters all the time.

to stick to it, making it look dirty. Then it's time for a bath! Use a gentle antibacterial soap made for people. (Dog shampoos are made for cleaning dogs' *hair.*) You don't need to bathe your dog too often—just when it gets yucky. Too much bathing dries out the skin and can cause skin problems. You want to keep your dog's skin silky and smooth.

4

Training Your Dog

Dogs are very smart. They can learn their name. They can also learn a lot of commands, including "come," "sit," and "stay." Some dogs can even roll over and play dead! But training isn't all about teaching tricks. Actually, training is *very* important. It teaches your dog to be a good pet.

Without good training, a dog can turn your house into a disaster area. A dog needs to learn how to behave, even when you're not home. Training takes time, however. Don't expect it to happen overnight. The best thing you can do is to spend time with your dog. When your dog learns to trust you, it will be easier to train.

You can train your dog to do all sorts of tricks.

Far Out!

Leader of the Pack

In the wild, dogs live in small groups, called packs. The members of the pack live and hunt together. They may also share in the care and feeding of the young. Every pack has a leader, called the alpha dog. The alpha dog is smart, able to lead the hunt, and gives protection for its members. The alpha dog is a strong, confident leader.

Dogs make good pets because they see their human owners as their pack. So they give them their loyalty and affection. Normally, a pet dog sees its main caretaker as the alpha dog. Sometimes, however, the dog may try to take over the position of alpha dog in a human family. It does what it wants to do and becomes out of control. The owner must be firm and make it clear who the "leader of the pack" is.

Crate Training

What do you do when your puppy keeps peeing on the floor? Or it keeps chewing up everything in sight? You're left cleaning up its mess. You might consider crate training. Using a crate is not a form of punishment. You do not put your pet in a crate because it has been a "bad puppy."

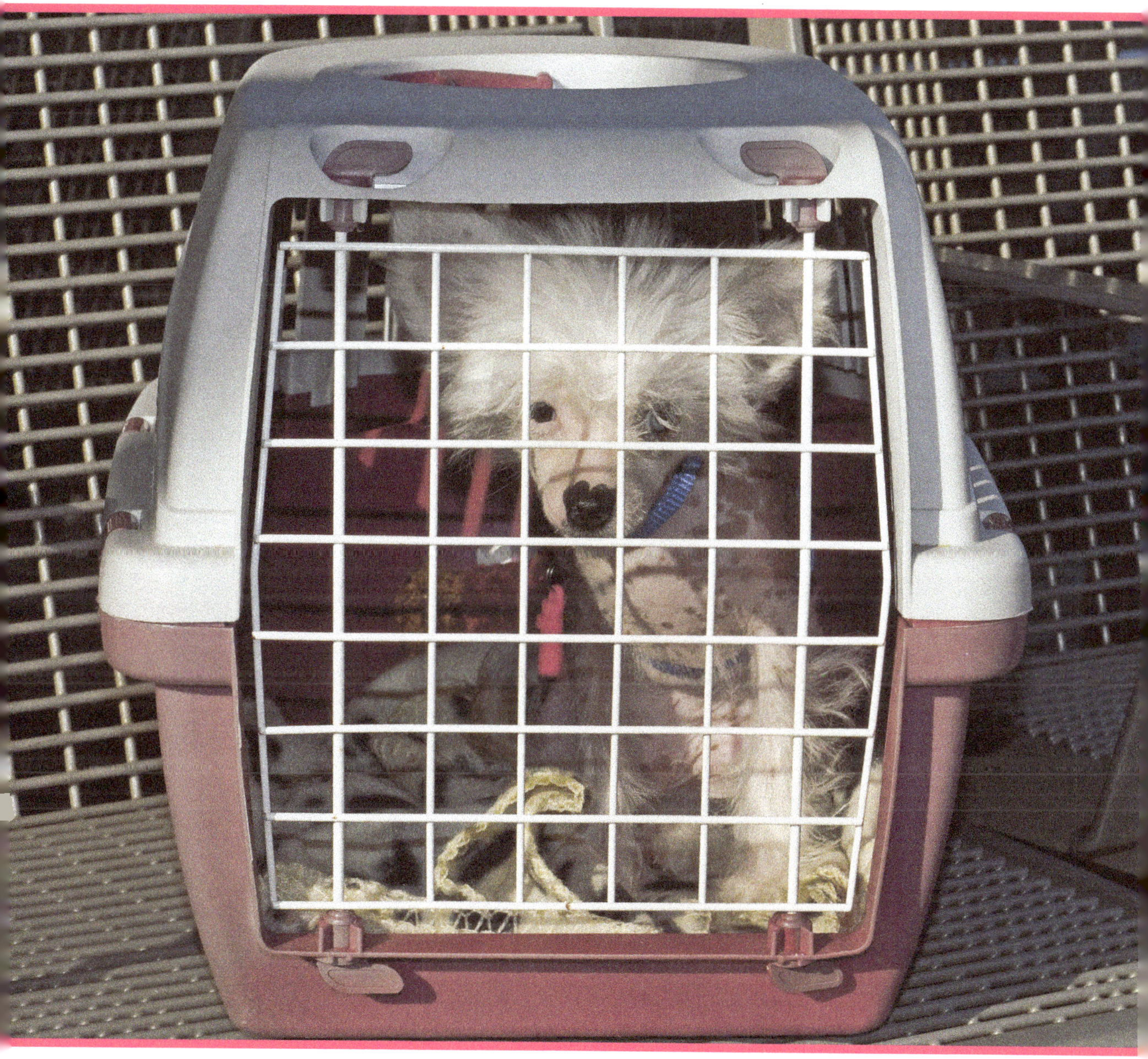

You can use a crate to help train your puppy. Keep your puppy in the crate during the day when nobody's home, and at night, too.

A crate is actually more like a place for comfort. It is like a "den," a place where dogs in the wild would go to sleep.

The crate keeps the puppy from destroying your home. It also helps with housebreaking. Keep your puppy in the crate during the day when nobody's home. When you get home, take your pet outside right away to do its business. You should keep the puppy in the crate at night, too, when everyone is sleeping. Otherwise, you will probably wake up to an "accident" on the floor. (Young puppies can't wait more than two or three hours before they have to "go.") Cleanup will be easier if you put a litter box inside the crate. You can train your dog to "go potty" there.

You will no longer need the crate when the puppy "asks" to go outside and no longer has accidents in the house. Another sign that your puppy is well-trained is when it no longer chews things that it is not supposed to.

Trick and Treat

The best way to train a dog is to give it treats. Food makes the perfect treat. You may use tiny bits of cooked chicken, dog biscuits, or something else your dog really likes. Whenever your pet does what you want it to, reward it with a treat. Repeat your commands over and over to help it learn. Give your dog lots of praise, too, when it does something right. Dogs love attention.

It is especially important to teach your dog the word "no." This can be helpful when it's chewing something it's not supposed to. Use a firm tone when you scold your dog and take it away from the forbidden object. Then give it a chew toy instead. Otherwise, you'll find it chewing on the furniture or your favorite sneakers again later.

Almost all puppies or dogs sometimes chew on things you wish they wouldn't. Don't worry about it too much. With good training and a lot of patience, you can teach your pet right from wrong. Eventually, your dog will figure it out and you

Love your pet, and it will love you back!

won't have to worry about it anymore. In the meantime, you can enjoy the endless love a hairless dog will give you. Your unusual pet will be a part of your family for a long time—twelve to fourteen years or more!

Words to Know

acne—A skin condition in which clogged oil pores become infected with bacteria, producing pimples.

allergy—The body's overreaction to a normally harmless substance, resulting in a rash, sneezing, breathing problems, or other symptoms.

alpha dog—The leader in a dog pack.

bacteria—Microscopic organisms; some bacteria can cause illness.

breed—A group of animals with similar characteristics produced by careful choice of the parents; also to mate animals and raise their young.

crest—Tuft of hair on top of a Chinese Crested's head.

dander—Flakes of dead skin.

pack—A group of wild animals that live and hunt together.

plume—A hairless dog's furry tail.

pore—An opening in the skin from which oil or sweat pours out.

socks—The fur-covered paws of a hairless dog.

Learn More

Books

Fernandez, Amy. *Xoloitzcuintli*. Freehold, N.J.: Kennel Club Books, 2009.

Mehus-Roe, Kristin. *Dogs for Kids! Everything You Need to Know About Dogs*. Irvine, Calif.: BowTie Press, 2007.

Morton, Anna. *Chinese Cresteds*. Hauppauge, N.Y.: Barron's Educational Series, Inc., 2007.

Web Sites

American Chinese Crested Club
<http://accc.chinesecrestedclub.info/>

American Hairless Terrier Association
<http://www.ahta.info>

American Kennel Club
<http://www.akc.org/>

Index